contents

4

7

10

12

14

16

18

Great Lakes

20

Rocky Mountains

22

New England Autumn

24

Pebble Beach

26

Santa Fe Tapestry

28

Canyonlands

Fields of **Sunflowers**

YARN

Lion Brand® Yarns *Heartland*, 5oz/142g balls, each approx 251yd/230m (acrylic)
• 6 balls in #136-174 Joshua Tree (A)
• 4 balls in #136-158 Yellowstone (B)
• 2 balls in #136-135 Yosemite (C)

HOOK
• Size I-9 (5.5mm) hook
  OR SIZE TO OBTAIN GAUGE

NOTIONS
• Lion Brand® large-eyed blunt needle

FINISHED MEASUREMENTS
Approx 51 x 68"/129.5 x 173cm

GAUGE
12 sts and 16 rows = 4"/10cm square over single crochet using size I-9 (5.5mm) hook.
Block measures 8"/20.5cm square.
TAKE TIME TO CHECK YOUR GAUGE.

ADJUSTABLE RING
1. To begin, wrap the yarn loosely around 2 fingers, the loose tail near your fingertips and the working yarn to the inside.
2. With the crochet hook, bring the working strand under the outside strand, then draw a loop through.
3. Draw through another loop to complete the single crochet. When all the stitches called for have been worked into the ring, close the ring by pulling the loose tail.

SUNFLOWER BLOCK
(make 42)

Rnd 1 With C, ch 6, join with sl st to form a ring, ch 2 (counts as dc), 23 dc in ring, join with sl st in top of ch, fasten off—24 dc.

Rnd 2 Join B with sl st in any st, ch 4 (counts as dc, ch 2), dc in same st as join, ch 1, [sk 2 dc, (dc, ch 2, dc) in next st, ch 1] 7 times, join with sl st in 2nd ch of beg ch—8 petals.

Rnd 3 Ch 3, (tr, ch 2, 2 tr) in 1st ch-2 sp, [sc in ch-1 sp, (2 tr, ch 2, 2 tr) in next ch-2 sp] 7 times, sc in last ch-1 sp, join with sl st in 2nd ch of beg ch.

Rnd 4 [(3 dc, ch 1, 3 dc) in ch-2 sp, sc in next sc] 8 times, join with sl st in 1st dc, fasten off.

Rnd 5 Join A with sl st in next ch-sp, [ch 4, hdc in next sc, ch 4, sc in ch-1 sp on next petal, ch 4, tr in next sc, ch 4, sc in ch-1 sp] 4 times, ending with sc in beg sp, join with sl st in 1st st of ch-4.

Rnd 6 Ch 3, 3 dc in ch-4 sp, dc in next hdc, 4 dc in next ch-4 sp, [3 dc in next ch-4 sp, 3 tr in next tr (corner made), 3 dc in next ch-4 sp, 4 dc in next ch-4 sp, dc in next hdc, 3 dc in next ch-4 sp] 3 times, ending with 3 dc in ch-4 sp, 3 tr in next tr, 3 dc in next ch-4 sp, join with sl st in 3rd ch of beg ch.

Rnd 7 Ch 2, [hdc in each dc, hdc in 1st tr, 3 dc in next tr, hdc in last tr] 3 times, ending with hdc in last 4 dc, join with sl st in 2nd ch of beg ch.

Rnd 8 Ch 1, sc in same st as join, sc in each st around, working 3 sc in center st of each corner, join with sl st in 1st sc, fasten off.

FINISHING
Whip st tog in a rectangle of 7 x 6 blocks.

SMALL FLOWER STRIP
(make 2)
Flower 1

Rnd 1 With C, using an adjustable ring, ch 3 (counts as hdc), 15 hdc in ring, join with sl st in 3rd ch of beg ch, fasten off, close ring—16 hdc.

Rnd 2 Join B with a sl st in any st, ch 3, (dc, ch 1, 2 dc) in same sp as join, sl st in next hdc, [(2 dc, ch 1, 2 dc) in next st, sl st in next hdc] 7 times, join with sl st in top of beg ch, fasten off—8 petals.

Fields of Sunflowers

Flowers 2–16

Rnd 1 Work as for Flower 1.
Rnd 2 Join B with a sl st in any st, ch 3, (dc, ch 1, 2 dc) in same sp as join, sl st in next hdc, [(2 dc, with WS tog, sl st through ch-1 sp of petal of previous flower, 2 dc) in next st, sl st in next hdc] twice, [(2 dc, ch 1, 2 dc) in next st, sl st in next hdc] 5 times, join with sl st in top of ch, fasten off—8 petals.

FINISHING

Block pieces lightly.

Attach Strips

Row 1 (RS) Join C in center sc of corner, ch 1, sc in each st across a shorter edge of afghan, turn—133 sc.
Row 2 Ch 1, sc in each of 1st 5 sc, [with RS tog, sc through next sc and ch-1 sp of petal, sc in next 3 sc] 32 times, sc in last 2 sc, fasten off.
Row 3 (Join second side of Flower Strip) With C, ch 134, sc in 2nd ch from hook and next 4 ch, sc through next ch and through WS of ch-1 sp of petal, sc in next 3 ch] 32 times, sc in last 2 ch, turn—133 sc.
Row 4 (RS) Ch 1, sc in each sc across, fasten off.
Ends (RS) (Side of Flower strip) Join A in 1st sc of row 2, ch 3, dc in ch-1 sp of petal, ch 3, dc in ch-1 sp of next petal, ch 3, join with sl st in base of 1st sc of row 3, fasten off. Rep for opposite end joining yarn in row 3 and ending in end of row 2.
Row 5 (RS) Join A in row 4 with a sl st, ch 1, sc in each st across, turn.
Row 6 Ch 1, sc in each st across, fasten off.
Rep for opposite end of afghan.

Border

With RS facing, attach A at the top right-hand corner in center sc of corner.
Rnd 1 (RS) Ch 1, sc evenly around afghan, working 3 sc in each corner, join with sl st in 1st sc.
Rnd 2 Ch 1, [sc in each of next 4 sc, ch-3, sl st in 3rd ch from hook for picot] around, working 2 sc in each corner, join with sl st in 1st sc, fasten off. ■

by Robyn Chachula

Mountain Streams

YARN
Lion Brand® Yarns *Heartland*, 5oz/142g balls, each approx 251yd/230m (acrylic)
- 3 balls in #136-105 Glacier Bay (A)
- 5 balls in #136-173 Everglades (B)

HOOK
- Size K-10.5 (6.5mm) hook
  OR SIZE TO OBTAIN GAUGE

NOTIONS
- Lion Brand® large-eyed blunt needle

FINISHED MEASUREMENTS
Approx 63 x 53½"/160 x 136cm

GAUGE
12 sts and 11 rows = 4"/10cm over pattern using size K-10.5 (6.5mm) hook.
TAKE TIME TO CHECK YOUR GAUGE.

STITCH GLOSSARY
Single Crochet Spike (sc spike) Insert hook in next st 3 rows below and pull up a loop, yo and pull through all the loops on hook.
X-Stitch (X-st) [Yo] 3 times, insert hook in indicated st, yo, pull up a lp, yo, draw through 2 lps on hook, yo, sk next st, insert hook in next st, yo, pull up a lp, yo, draw through 2 lps on hook, yo, draw through 3 lps, yo, draw through 2 lps, yo, draw through last 2 lps, ch 1, dc in middle of horizontal bar of st just made (where the bottom legs of the st intersect).
Y-Stitch (Y-st) Dtr in st indicated, [ch 1, dc into middle of horizontal bar of st just made] 3 times.

P-Stitch (P-st) Dtr in st indicated, ch 1, dc into middle of horizontal bar of st just made.

NOTES
Change color by working to last 2 loops of last stitch of row, drop the old color, pick up the new color and draw it through the remaining 2 loops on the hook. Carry the unused color along edge at the beginning of wrong side rows.

AFGHAN
With A, ch 142.
Row 1 (RS) Sc in 2nd ch from hook, * sc in next ch, hdc in next ch, dc in each of next 5 ch, hdc in next ch, sc in next ch **, ch 1, sk next ch; rep from * across

to last ch ending at **, sc in last sc, change to B, turn—141 sts.
Row 2 (WS) Ch 1, sc in 1st sc, [sc in each of next 9 sts, sc spike over ch-sp into ch st 2 rows below] 13 times, sc in each of last 10 sts, turn.
Row 3 Ch 1, sc in each sc across, change to A, turn.
Row 4 Ch 3 (counts as dc), [dc in each of next 2 sc, hdc in next sc, sc in next sc, ch 1, sk 1 sc, sc in next sc, hdc in next sc, dc in each of next 3 sc] 14 times, turn.
Row 5 Ch 3 (counts as dc), [dc in each of next 2 dc, hdc in next hdc, sc in next sc, ch 1, sk ch-sp, sc in next sc, hdc in next hdc, dc in each of next 3 dc] 14 times, change to B, turn.

by Robyn Chachula

Mountain **Streams**

Row 6 Ch 1, sc in first sc, [sc in each of next 4 sc, sc spike over ch-sp into sc 3 rows below, sc in each of next 5 sc] 14 times, sc in top of t-ch, turn.

Row 7 Rep Row 3.

Row 8 Ch 1, sc in 1st sc, [sc in next sc, hdc in next sc, dc in each of next 5 sc, hdc in next sc, sc in next sc *, ch 1, sk next sc] 14 times, ending last rep at *, sc in last sc, turn.

Row 9 Ch 1, sc in 1st sc, [sc in next sc, hdc in next hdc, dc in each of next 5 dc, hdc in next hdc, sc in next sc *, ch 1, sk ch-sp] 14 times, ending last rep at *, sc in last sc, change to B, turn.

Row 10 Ch 1, sc in 1st sc, [sc in each of next 9 sts, sc spike over ch-sp into sc 3 rows below] 13 times, sc in each of last 10 sts, turn.

Rep rows 3–10 eighteen times more, then rep rows 3–7 once.

Next row Ch 1, sc in first sc, [sc in next sc, hdc in next sc, dc in each of next 5 sc, hdc in next sc, sc in each of next 2 sc] 14 times, change to B, fasten off A.

EDGING

Rnd 1 (RS) Ch 1, sc in each st across, * 3 sc in corner, work 161 sc evenly spaced along ends of rows, 3 sc in corner **, working into foundation ch, sc in each st across; rep from * to **, sl st in 1st sc, turn.

Rnd 2 Ch 1, sc in 1st sc, [3 sc in corner sc, sc in each sc across to corner] 4 times, sl st in 1st sc, turn.

Rnd 3 Sl st in 1st sc, ch 2, sk 1 sc, P-st in next sc, * [X-st over next 3 sc] across to corner sc **, Y-st in corner sc, X-st in corner sc and next 2 sts; rep from * 3 times more ending last rep at **, sl st in top of P-st, turn.

Rnd 4 Ch 1, 3 sc in ch-1 sp of each X-st around, sl st in 1st sc, turn.

Rnd 5 Sl st in next sc, rep rnd 3.

Rnd 6 Rep rnd 4.

Rnd 7 Ch 1, [sc in each sc to corner, 3 sc in corner] 4 times, sl st in 1st sc, fasten off. ▪

Aspen **Snowfall**

YARN (4)

Lion Brand® Yarns *Heartland*, 5oz/142g balls, each approx 251yd/230m (acrylic)
• 8 balls in #136-098 Acada

HOOK

• Size J-10 (6mm) hook
  OR SIZE TO OBTAIN GAUGE

NOTIONS

• Stitch marker
• Lion Brand® large-eyed blunt needle

FINISHED MEASUREMENTS

Approx 47 x 61"/119.5 x 155cm

GAUGE

11 sts and 14 rows = 4"/10cm over single crochet using size J-10 hook. Motif measures 4¼"/11cm in diameter. *TAKE TIME TO CHECK YOUR GAUGE.*

ADJUSTABLE RING

1. To begin, wrap the yarn loosely around 2 fingers, the loose tail near your fingertips and the working yarn to the inside.
2. With the crochet hook, bring the working strand under the outside strand, then draw a loop through.
3. Draw through another loop to complete the single crochet. When all the stitches called for have been worked into the ring, close the ring by pulling the loose tail.

STITCH GLOSSARY

Dcbl (double crochet back loop) Dc into the back loop only.
Scbl (single crochet back loop) Sc into the back loop only.

Joining Work to point of first join, insert hook under both loops in sc of motif being joined to, insert hook through the back loop only on the motif in progress, yo and pull through all 4 loops on hook. All joins consist of 4 consecutive sts with 5 skipped sts between joins.

NOTES

Afghan is worked in circular motifs. Circles are joined to afghan as the last round is completed. Starting chains on rounds are not counted as stitches and are not worked into.

ROW 1
Motif A

Make an adjustable ring.
Rnd 1 Ch 2, 12 dc in ring, sl st to 1st dc to join—12 dc.
Rnd 2 Ch 1, [2 sc in next st, sc in next st] 6 times, sl st to 1st sc to join—18 sc.
Rnd 3 Ch 2, [2 dcbl in next st] 18 times, sl st to 1st dc to join—36 st.
Rnd 4 Ch 1, scbl in each st around, sl st to 1st sc to join, fasten off.
Note Place a marker in this circle. Keep this oriented as the top left corner throughout for consistency in the direction of all joins.

Motif B

Rnds 1–3 Work as for Motif A.
Rnd 4 Ch 1, scbl in next 30 sts, join to any 4 sts on Motif A, sc in last 2 sts, sl st to 1st sc to join, fasten off.

Motif C (rep 9 times)

Rnds 1–3 Work as for Motif A.
Rnd 4 Ch 1, scbl in next 30 sts, sk first 12 sc on last rnd of previous motif, join to next 4 sts on previous motif, sc in last 2 sts, sl st to 1st sc to join, fasten off.

ROWS 2–14
Motif D

Rnds 1–3 Work as for Motif A.
Rnd 4 Ch 1, scbl in next 30 sts, beg 9 sts before join bet 1st 2 motifs of last row, join to next 4 sts, sc in last 2 sts, sl st to 1st sc to join, fasten off.

Motif E (rep 10 times)

Rnds 1–3 Work as for Motif A.
Rnd 4 Ch 1, sc in next 21 sts, sk 5 sts on next motif in previous row, join to next 4 sts, sc in next 5 sts, beg 9 sts before join of previous motif in same row with previous row, join to next 4 sts, sc in next 2 sts, sl st to 1st sc to join, fasten off.

EDGING

Rnd 1 Sk 1 st after last join, attach yarn with a sl st in back lp of next sc, [scbl to 1 st before next join, sk 1 st before and after each join] around, sl st in 1st sc to join—588 sc.
Rnd 2 Ch 1, scbl in each st around, skipping 2 sts at each join, sl st in first sc to join, fasten off—496 sc. ∎

Appalachian Trail

YARN 🄴

Lion Brand® Yarns *Heartland*, 5oz/142g balls, each approx 251yd/230m (acrylic)
- 2 balls in #136-098 Acadia (A)
- 2 balls in #136-173 Everglades (B)
- 1 ball in #136-174 Joshua Tree (C)
- 1 ball in #136-126 Sequoia (D)

HOOK

- Size J-10 (6mm) hook
  OR SIZE TO OBTAIN GAUGE

NOTIONS

- Lion Brand® large-eyed blunt needle

■■■□

FINISHED MEASUREMENTS

Approx 45 x 60"/114.5 x 152.5cm, excluding fringe

GAUGES

12 sts and 7 rows = approx 4"/10cm over stitch pattern.
One stitch pattern repeat = approx 12"/30.5cm long.
11 dc and 7 rows = 4¼"/11cm.
TAKE TIME TO CHECK YOUR GAUGES.

NOTES

The afghan is worked lengthwise. The beginning and the end tails will be used as fringe, so when you start and end a row, leave long ends (about 9"/23cm or more) to incorporate into the fringe. There is no Right Side (RS) or Wrong Side (WS) to this afghan. One pattern repeat is worked on 11 dc eyelets at the beginning. To make your afghan longer or shorter, add or subtract 11 dc eyelets of the foundation, to add or subtract approx 12"/30.5cm

STITCH GLOSSARY

Dc eyelet Ch 4, dc in 4th ch from the hook.
3dc2tog (worked over 2 spaces or eyelets) 2 dc in indicated sp, dc2tog over same sp as last 2 sts and next sp, 2 dc in same sp—5 sts.

AFGHAN

Row 1 With A, leaving a long tail, ch 4, dc in 4th ch from hook (1 dc eyelet made), [ch 5, dc in 4th ch from hook] 55 times, turn—56 dc eyelets.

Row 2 Ch 4 (counts as [dc, ch-1] here and following), 3 dc in 1st dc eyelet, ch 1, (3 dc, ch 1) in each of next 4 dc eyelets, 3dc2tog in next 2 dc eyelets, ch 1, (3 dc, ch 1) in each of next 4 dc eyelets, [(3 dc, ch 1) twice in next dc eyelet, (3 dc, ch 1) in each of next 4 dc eyelets, 3dc2tog in next 2 dc eyelets, ch 1, (3 dc, ch 1) in each of next 4 dc eyelets] 4 times, (3 dc, ch 1, dc) in last dc eyelet. Fasten off A, leaving long tail, turn.
Row 3 Join B, leaving long tail, ch 4, (3 dc, ch 1) in 1st ch-1 sp, (3 dc, ch 1) in each of next 4 ch-1 sps, 3dc2tog in next 2 ch-1 sps, ch 1, (3 dc, ch 1) in each of next 4 ch-1 sps, [(3 dc, ch 1) twice in next ch-1 sp, (3 dc, ch 1) in each of next 4 ch-1 sps, 3dc2tog in next 2 ch-1 sps, ch 1, (3 dc, ch 1) in each of next 4 ch-1 sps] 4 times, (3 dc, ch 1, dc) in last ch-1 sp. Fasten off B, leaving long tail, turn.
Row 4 Join C, leaving long tail, rep row 3.
Row 5 Join D, leaving long tail, rep row 3.
Rows 6–53 Rep row 3, using yarns A, B, C, D in that order, 12 times.

FINISHING
Fringe

Make 52 fringe for each straight edge as foll: cut 5 strands of A 17"/43.2cm long, fold in half and pull loop through sp at end of Row 2 catching the tail, pull ends through loop to knot fringe. Rep in each sp across with color to match row. Rep for opposite end. Trim ends to even length. ■

Garden State Pansies

YARN (4)

Lion Brand® Yarns *Heartland*, 5oz/142g balls, each approx 251yd/230m (acrylic)
- 2 balls in #136-147 Hot Springs (A)
- 2 balls in #136-103 Denali (B)
- 2 balls in #136-169 Shenandoah (C)

HOOK

- Size J-10 (6 mm) hook
  OR SIZE TO OBTAIN GAUGE

NOTIONS

- Lion Brand® large-eyed blunt needle

FINISHED MEASUREMENTS

Approx 35 x 44"/89 x 112cm

GAUGE

12 sts and 15 rows = 4"/10cm over single crochet with size J-10 (6 mm) hook.
One motif measures approx 4½"/11.5cm square.
TAKE TIME TO CHECK YOUR GAUGE.

PANSY MOTIF

(make 63)
With A, ch 5, sl st in 1st st to form a ring.
Rnd 1 Ch 3, [5 dc, ch 5] 4 times in ring, join with sl st in 1st dc, fasten off—4 petals.
Rnd 2 Join B with sl st in ring,* sc over ch-5 and into ring, ch 3, [dc in next dc, 2 dc in next dc] twice, dc in next dc, ch 3; rep from * 3 times more, join with sl st in 1st sc, fasten off.
Rnd 3 Join C with sl st in any sc, ch 4, * dc in next dc, 2 dc in next dc, 2 tr in each of next 3 dc, 2 dc in next dc, dc in next dc, ch 4, sl st in next sc; rep from * once more, fasten off.

ASSEMBLY

Join 9 motifs for each strip as foll: join rnd 2 of one motif to row 3 of next motif so motifs are facing in the same direction (see photo). Rep for a total of 7 strips. Join strips, alternating direction of motifs, attaching sides of rnd 2 of one motif to sides of row 3 of next motif (see photo).

BORDER

Rnd 1 *First Side* With RS facing and motif at top right corner with row 3 on top, join A with sl st in same sc as join at beg of row 3 (at right edge of corner). Ch 6 (counts as tr, ch 2), sc in next 3 dc, * ch 2, sk 3 tr, sc in next tr, ch 2, sk 2 tr, sc in each of next 3 dc, ch 2, tr in next sc, ch 2, sc in each of next 3 dc, ch 2, sk 2 tr, sc in next tr, ch 2 **, tr in join bet motifs, ch 2, sk 4 sts of rnd 2 of next motif, sc in next dc, ch 2, dc in next sc, ch 2, sk ch and next dc, sc in next dc, ch 2, tr in join between motifs #; rep from * twice. Rep from * to **. *Second Side* Sc in each of next 3 tr, ch 2, tr in next sc, ch 2, sk ch and dc, dc in next dc, † ch 2, tr in join between motifs, ch 2, sk 3 sts in row 3 petal, sc in next tr, ch 2, sk 2 tr, sc in each of next 3 dc, ch 2, tr in next sc, ch 2, sk ch and dc, dc in next dc; rep from † 7 times. *Third Side* Ch 2, sk 2 dc, dc in next dc, ch 2, tr in next sc, ch 2, sk ch and dc, dc in next dc, ch 2, tr in join bet motifs; rep from * to # 3 times omitting last tr. *Fourth Side* [Sk 2 dc, dc in next dc, ch 2, tr in next sc, ch 2, sc in each of next 3 dc, ch 2, sk 3 tr, sc in next tr, ch 2, tr in join bet motifs, ch 2] 8 times omitting last tr, join with sl st in 4th st of beg-ch.
Rnd 2 Ch 1, [2 sc in each ch-sp, sc in each st] around, join with sl st in 1st sc to join, adjusting as needed to a multiple of 3 sts around, fasten off.
Rnd 3 Join B with sl st in any st, ch 1, sc in each st around, join with sl st in 1st sc, fasten off.
Rnd 4 Join C with sl st in any st, (sc, ch 3, 2 dc) in same st as join, * sk 2 sc, (sc, ch 3, 2 dc) in next sc; rep from * around, join with sl st in 1st sc, fasten off. ■

by Jennifer J. Cirka

Oregon Trail

YARN (4)

Lion Brand® Yarns *Heartland*, 5oz/142g balls, each approx 251yd/230m (acrylic)
- 2 balls in #136-147 Hot Springs (A)
- 2 balls in #136-109 Olympic (B)
- 1 ball in #136-113 Redwood (C)
- 1 ball in #136-169 Shenandoah (D)
- 2 balls in #136-189 Isle Royale (E)
- 2 balls in #136-135 Yosemite (F)
- 1 ball in #136-149 Great Smoky Mountains (G)
- 1 ball in #136-158 Yellowstone (H)

HOOK

- Size K-10.5 (6.5mm) hook
  OR SIZE TO OBTAIN GAUGE

NOTIONS

- Lion Brand® large-eyed blunt needle

FINISHED MEASUREMENTS

Approx 50"/127cm in diameter

GAUGE

Rnds 1–3 = 5"/13cm in diameter.
TAKE TIME TO CHECK YOUR GAUGE.

NOTES

Afghan is worked in the round. Do not turn at the end of each round. Change to next color when joining at the end of rounds by working to the last 2 loops of the last stitch of the round, cut the old color, pick up the new color and draw through remaining 2 loops on the hook.

STITCH GLOSSARY

Beg cl (Beginning Cluster) Ch 2, [yo, insert hook in ch-sp and pull up a lp, yo and draw through 2 lps on hook] 2 times, yo and draw through rem 3 lps on hook.

Cl (Cluster) [Yo, insert hook in ch-sp and pull up a lp, yo and draw through 2 lps on hook] 3 times, yo and draw through rem 4 lps on hook.

AFGHAN

With A, ch 6, join with sl st to form a ring.

Rnd 1 Beg cl, ch 2, [Cl, ch 2] 7 times in ring, joining B in last st, join with sl st in 1st ch-2 sp, fasten off A—8 Cl.

Rnd 2 Beg cl, ch 2, Cl in same ch-2 sp, [ch 1, (Cl, ch 2, Cl) in next ch-2 sp] 7 times, joining C in last st, join with sl st in 1st ch-2 sp, fasten off B—16 Cl.

Rnd 3 (Beg cl, ch 2, Cl, ch 1) in same ch-2 sp as joining, (Cl, ch 1) in ch-1 sp, [(Cl, ch 2, Cl, ch 1) in next ch-2 sp, (Cl, ch 1) in next ch-1 sp] 7 times, joining D in last st, join with sl st in 1st ch-2 sp, fasten off C—24 Cl.

Rnd 4 (Beg cl, ch 2, Cl, ch 1) in same ch-2 sp as joining, (Cl, ch 1) in each ch-1 sp, [(Cl, ch 2, Cl, ch 1) in next ch-2 sp, (Cl, ch 1) in each ch-1 sp] 7 times, joining C in last st, join with sl st in 1st ch-2 sp, fasten of D—32 Cl.

Rnds 5–35 Rep rnd 4, inc 8 Cl each rnd in stripe pat as foll:
B, E, B, E, F, G, A, F, E, B, C, A, G, D, C, H, B, A, G, D, G, E, F, H, B, E, A, H, F, E, B
Join C at end of last rnd.

Trim

Rnd 36 Ch 1, * 3 sc in ch-2 sp, [sc in next Cl, sc in next ch-1 sp] 33 times; rep from * 7 times more, join with sl st in 1st sc, fasten off. ■

by Ellen Liguori

Great Lakes

YARN
Lion Brand® Yarns *Heartland*, 5oz/142g balls, each approx 251yd/230m (acrylic)
• 8 balls in #136-109 Olympic

HOOK
• Size J-10 (6mm) hook
OR SIZE TO OBTAIN GAUGE

NOTIONS
• Lion Brand® large-eyed blunt needle

FINISHED MEASUREMENTS
Approx 50 x 60"/127 x 152.5cm

GAUGE
14 sts and 18 rows = 4"/10cm square over sc using size J-10 (6mm) crochet hook. *TAKE TIME TO CHECK YOUR GAUGE.*

STITCH GLOSSARY
3 dc Cl (cluster) [Yo, insert hook in next stitch, yo, pull up lp, yo, draw through 2 lps on hook] 3 times, yo, draw through all 4 lps on hook.

4 dc Cl [Yo, insert hook in next stitch, yo, pull up lp, yo, draw through 2 lps on hook] 4 times, yo, draw through all 5 lps on hook.

7 dc Cl [Yo, insert hook in next stitch, yo, pull up lp, yo, draw through 2 lps on hook] 7 times, yo, draw through all 8 lps on hook.

AFGHAN
Ch 147.

Row 1 3 dc Cl over 4th, 5th and 6th ch from hook, * ch 1, [tr in next ch, ch 1] twice, (tr, ch 1, tr) in next ch, [ch 1, 1 tr in next ch] twice, ch 1, 7 dc Cl; rep from * work 4 dc Cl over last 4 ch, turn—12 arches.

Row 2 Ch 3, dc in ch-sp, * [dc in tr, dc in ch-sp] 5 times, dc in next tr, dc2tog in next 2 ch-sp; rep from * 11 times more, end with dc2tog over last ch-sp and last Cl, turn—145 dc.

Row 3 Ch 3, 3 dc Cl over next 3 dc, * ch 1, [tr in next dc, ch 1] twice, (tr, ch 1, tr) in next dc, [ch 1, tr in next dc] twice, ch 1, 7 dc Cl; rep from * across, end with 4 dc Cl over last 4 dc, turn.
Rep rows 2–3 until afghan measures approximately 58"/147.5cm, end with row 3.

FINISHING
Border
Rnd 1 Rotate to work in ends of rows, ch 3 (counts as dc), dc evenly spaced along side, 5 dc in corner. Rotate to work across foundation row, dc in next 4 ch-sp, * 3 dc Cl in next 3 ch-sp, dc in next 9 ch-sp; rep from *, end with dc in last 4 ch-sp, 5 dc in corner. Rotate to work dc evenly spaced along side, 5 dc in corner. Rotate to work across top row, * dc in next 11 dc, 3 dc Cl in next 3 dc; rep from * to last 2 dc, dc2tog, join with sl st in top of ch-3, turn.

Rnd 2 Ch 1, sc in each dc around, join with sl st in 1st sc, turn.

Rnd 3 Sl st in each sc around, working in front loops only, join with sl st in 1st sl st, fasten off. ■

Rocky **Mountains**

YARN ④

Lion Brand® Yarns *Heartland*, 5oz/142g balls, each approx 251yd/230m (acrylic)
• 6 balls in #136-098 Acadia (A)
• 6 balls in #136-109 Olympic (B)

HOOK

• Size I-9 (5.50 mm) hook
OR SIZE TO OBTAIN GAUGE

NOTIONS

• Lion Brand® large-eyed blunt needle

FINISHED MEASUREMENTS

Approx 50 x 61"/127 x 155cm

GAUGE

12 sts and 16 rows = 4"/10cm over pattern using size I-9 (5.50 mm) hook.
TAKE TIME TO CHECK YOUR GAUGE.

NOTES

Work all dc sts in front of ch-2 spaces. Change color by working to the last 2 loops of the last stitch of the row, drop the old color, then pick up new color and draw through 2 loops on hook. Carry the unused color along edge.

STITCH GLOSSARY

Rev sc (reverse single crochet) Working left to right (or right to left if you are left handed), insert hook in next stitch to the right (left), pull up a lp, yo and draw through 2 lps on hook.

AFGHAN

With A, ch 148.
Row 1 (RS) With A, sc in 2nd ch from hook and each ch across, turn—147 sc.

Row 2 (WS) Ch 1, sc in each sc across, changing to B in last st, turn.
Row 3 Ch 1, sc in 1st sc, [ch 2, skip next sc, sc in next sc, ch 2, skip next sc, sc in each of next 3 sc, ch 2, skip next sc, sc in next sc] 18 times, ch 2, skip next sc, sc in next sc, turn—202 sts (55 ch-2 sps, 92 sc).
Row 4 Ch 1, sc in 1st sc, [ch 2, skip next ch-2 sp, sc in next sc, ch 2, skip next ch-2 sp, sc in each of next 3 sc, ch 2, skip next ch-2 sp, sc in next sc] 18 times, ch 2, skip next ch-2 sp, sc in last sc, changing to A, turn.
Row 5 Ch 1, sc in 1st sc, [dc in next skipped sc 3 rows below, sc in next sc, dc in next skipped sc 3 rows below, ch 2, skip next sc, sc in next sc, ch 2, skip the next sc, dc in next skipped sc 3 rows below, sc in next sc] 18 times, dc in next skipped sc 3 rows below, sc in last sc, turn.
Row 6 Ch 1, sc in each of next 4 sts, [ch 2, skip next ch-2 sp, sc in next sc, ch 2, skip next ch-2 sp, sc in each of next 5 sts] 18 times, ch 2, skip next ch-2 sp, sc in next sc, ch 2, skip next ch-2 sp, sc in each of next 4 sts, changing to B in last st, turn.
Row 7 Ch 1, sc in 1st sc, * ch 2, skip next sc, sc in each of next 2 sc, [dc in next skipped sc 3 rows below, sc in next sc] 2 times, sc in next sc; rep from * 17 more times, ch 2, skip next sc, sc in last sc, turn.
Row 8 Ch 1, sc in 1st sc, [ch 2, skip next ch-2 sp, sc in each of next 7 sts] 18 times, ch 2, skip next ch-2 sp, sc in last sc, changing to A, turn.
Row 9 Ch 1, sc in 1st sc, * dc in next skipped sc 3 rows below, [ch 2, skip next sc, sc in next sc] 3 times, ch 2, skip

next sc; rep from * 17 more times, dc in next skipped sc 3 rows below, sc in last sc, turn.
Row 10 Ch 1, sc in 1st 2 sts, [ch 2, skip next ch-2 sp, sc in next st] 72 times, sc in last sc, changing to B, turn.
Row 11 Ch 1, sc in each of 1st 2 sc, [dc in next skipped sc 3 rows below, sc in next st] 72 times, sc in last sc, turn.
Row 12 Ch 1, sc in each st across, changing to A in last st, turn.
Rows 13–22 As rows 3–12 except using reverse colors.
Rep rows 3–22 until piece measures approx 60"/152.5cm from beg, end after row 22. Do not fasten off.

BORDER

Rnd 1 (RS) With RS facing and A, ch 1, sc evenly around, working 3 sc in each corner, join with slip st in 1st sc.
Rnd 2 Ch 1, rev sc in each st around, join with slip st in 1st sc, fasten off. ■

New England **Autumn**

YARN

Lion Brand® Yarns *Heartland*, 5oz/142g balls, each approx 251yd/230m (acrylic)
- 1 ball in #136-158 Yellowstone (A)
- 1 ball in #136-135 Yosemite (B)
- 3 balls in #136-113 Redwood (C)
- 4 balls in #136-098 Acadia (D)
- 6 balls in #136-126 Sequoia (E)

HOOK
- Size J-10 (6mm) hook
  OR SIZE TO OBTAIN GAUGE

NOTIONS
- Lion Brand® large-eyed blunt needle

FINISHED MEASUREMENTS
Approx 53 x 66"/134.5 x 167.5cm

GAUGE
Rnds 1–2 = 2½"/6.5cm across;
6½"/16.5cm square = after blocking.
TAKE TIME TO CHECK YOUR GAUGE.

STITCH GLOSSARY
Scbl (single crochet back loop) Sc into the back loop only.
Hdcbl (half double crochet back loop) Hdc into the back loop only.

SQUARE
(make 80)
With A, ch 4, sl st in 4th ch from hook to form ring.
Rnd 1 Ch 3 (counts as dc), 15 dc in ring, join with sl st in top of ch-3, fasten off—16 dc.
Rnd 2 Join B in any st, ch 4 (counts as dc, ch 1), ([dc, ch 1] twice, dc) in same st, *sk next st, sc in next st, sk next st

**, ([dc, ch 1] 3 times dc) in next st; rep from * twice more, rep from * to **, join with sl st in 3rd ch of beg ch-4, fasten off—20 sts.
Rnd 3 Join C in any ch-1 corner sp, ch 3, (2 dc, ch 1, 3 dc) in same sp, * sk next dc, 2 dc in next sp, sk next dc, dc in next sc, sk next dc, 2 dc in next sp, sk next dc **, (3 dc, ch 1, 3 dc) in next ch-1 corner sp; rep from * twice more, rep from * to **, join with sl st in beg ch-3, fasten off—44 dc.
Rnd 4 Join D in any ch-1 corner sp, [(sc, ch 3, sc) in corner ch-1 sp, scbl in next 11 dc] 4 times, join with sl st in 1st sc—52 sc.
Rnd 5 Sl st in ch-3 corner sp, ch 3, (2 dc, ch 1, 3 dc) in same sp, * sk next sc, dc in next 11 sc, sk next sc **, (3 dc, ch 1, 3 dc) in next corner ch-3 sp; rep from * twice more; rep from * to **, join with sl st in top of beg ch-3, fasten off—68 dc.
Rnd 6 Join E in any ch-1 corner sp, [(sc, ch 3, sc) in corner, sc in next 17 dc] 4 times, join with sl st in 1st sc—76 sc.
Rnd 7 Sl st in ch-3 corner sp, ch 3, (2 dc, ch 1, 3 dc) in same sp, * sk next sc, dc in each of next 17 sc, sk next sc **, (3 dc, ch 1, 3 dc) in next corner ch-3 sp; rep from * twice more, rep from * to **, join with sl st in top of beg ch-3, fasten off—92 dc.

FINISHING
Block squares.

Assembly
Using E, whipstitch blocks tog with 8 blocks along the bottom edge, and 10 blocks along the side edge (use photo as guide).

Border
Rnd 1 Join E in any ch-1 corner sp, [(sc, ch 3, sc) in corner ch-1 sp, sc in each dc and joined corner sp to next corner] 4 times, join with sl st in 1st sc, fasten off.
Rnd 2 Join A in any ch-3 corner sp, [3 sc in corner ch-sp, scbl in each sc to next corner] 4 times, join with sl st in 1st sc, fasten off.
Rnd 3 Join C in any center corner sc, ch 2 (counts as hdc), 2 hdc in same st, [hdcbl in each st across to next corner, 3 hdc in corner st] 3 times, hdcbl in each st across to last corner, join with sl st in top of beg ch-2, fasten off. ■

Pebble Beach

By Jacqueline van Dillen

YARN (4)

Lion Brand® Yarns *Heartland*, 5oz/142g balls, each approx 251yd/230m (acrylic)
• 4 balls in #136-122 Grand Canyon (A)
• 4 balls in #136-098 Acada (B)

HOOK

• Size J-10 (6mm) hook
  OR SIZE TO OBTAIN GAUGE

NOTIONS

• Lion Brand® large-eyed blunt needle

FINISHED MEASUREMENTS

Approx 40 x 46"/101.5 x 117cm, excluding fringe

GAUGE

3 repeats and 10 rows = 4"/10cm over pattern using size J-10 (6mm) hook. *TAKE TIME TO CHECK YOUR GAUGE.*

STITCH GLOSSARY

Cl (cluster) * [Yo] twice, insert hook into designated stitch, yo, pull up a lp, [yo, draw through 2 lps on hook] twice; rep from * 4 times more, yo and draw through all 6 lps on hook, ch 1.

NOTES

Change colors by working to last 2 loops of last stitch of row, drop old color, pick up new color and draw through 2 loops on hook. Carry unused color along edge at the beginning of RS rows.

AFGHAN

With A, ch 170.
Row 1 (RS) Cl in 4th ch from hook, [ch 2, sk next 2 ch, sc in next sc, ch 2, sk next 2 ch, Cl in next ch] 27 times, ch 2, sk next 2 ch, sc in next ch, ch 1, dc in last ch, turn—28 Cl.

Row 2 (WS) Ch 1, [sc in next sc, ch 2, sc in Cl, ch 2] 27 times, sc in next sc, ch 2, sc in Cl, sc in top of t-ch changing to B, turn.
Row 3 Ch 3, sk 1 sc, [sc in next sc, ch 2, Cl in next sc, ch 2] 27 times, sc in next sc, ch 2, Cl in next sc, dc in t-ch, turn.
Row 4 [Ch 2, sc in Cl, ch 2, sc in next sc] 28 times, sc in top of t-ch changing to A, turn.
Row 5 Ch 3, [Cl in next sc, ch 2, sc in next sc, ch 2] 27 times, Cl in next sc, ch 2, sc in next sc, dc in t-ch, turn.
Rep rows 2–5 until work measures approx 46"/117cm from beg, ending with row 3.

FINISHING

Make 57 fringe for each short edge as foll: * cut 3 strands of B 12"/30.5cm long, fold strands in half and pull loop through ch-sp of foundation row, pull ends through loop to knot fringe; rep from * in each ch-sp across. Knot 3 strands from each fringe tog bet each knot. Knot 3 strands at each end. Rep with A in last row. ■

Santa Fe Tapestry

YARN

Lion Brand® Yarns *Heartland*, 5oz/142g balls, each approx 251yd/230m (acrylic)
- 5 balls in #136-098 Acadia (A)
- 5 balls in #136-153 Black Canyon (B)
- 1 ball in #136-105 Glacier Bay (C)
- 1 ball in #136-113 Redwood (D)
- 1 ball in #136-135 Yosemite (E)

HOOK

- Size 7 (4.5mm) hook
  OR SIZE TO OBTAIN GAUGE

NOTIONS

- Lion Brand® large-eyed blunt needle

FINISHED MEASUREMENTS

Approx 48 x 58"/122 x 147.5cm

GAUGE

16 sts and 8 rows = 4"/10cm over double crochet using size 7 (4.5mm) hook.
TAKE TIME TO CHECK YOUR GAUGE.

NOTES

Follow chart for color changes. Change color by working to last 2 loops of current stitch, drop old color, yarn over with new color and pull through remaining loops on hook to complete the stitch. Carry unused color along back of work, working over the yarn on the next row.

AFGHAN

With E, ch 194.
Row 1 Dc in 4th ch from hook and each ch across—192 dc.

Beg chart

Rows 2–57 Beg at row 2 in dc, work 32-st chart rep 6 times over 192 dc.

Reverse chart

Rows 58–114 Beg at row 57 and 1st st, work 32-st chart rep 6 times over 192 dc from top to bottom. Fasten off.

FINISHING

With RS facing and A & B held tog, join with sl st in top of t-ch, *ch 3, sc in each of next 18 sts, sk 1 st; rep from * across, ending with ch 3, sc in last dc—11 ch-3 sps. Rep along bottom edge.

Fringe

* Cut 6 strands of yarn 25"/63.5 cm long in any random color combination. Fold strands in half to form a loop, draw loop through ch-sp to WS, pull yarn ends through loop and tighten. Braid fringe 4–5"/10.2–12.7cm long and knot end to secure, trim ends; rep from * for each ch-sp across on top and bottom edges. ■

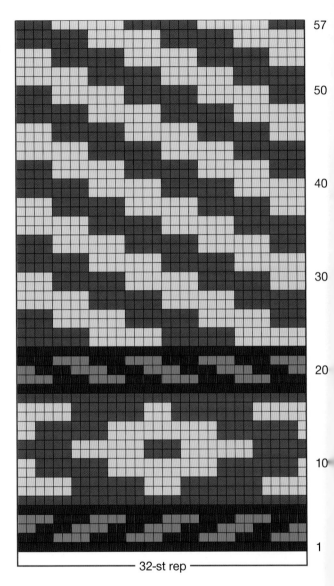

32-st rep

COLOR KEY

- ☐ Acadia (A)
- ■ Black Canyon (B)
- ■ Glacier Bay (C)
- ■ Redwood (D)
- ■ Yosemite (E)

Canyonlands

YARN

Lion Brand® Yarns *Heartland*, 5oz/142g balls, each approx 251yd/230m (acrylic)
• 4 balls in #136-098 Acadia (A)
• 1 ball in #136-135 Yellowstone (B)
• 1 ball in #136-135 Yosemite (C)

HOOK

• Size J-10 (6mm) hook
  OR SIZE TO OBTAIN GAUGE

NOTIONS

• Lion Brand® large-eyed blunt needle

FINISHED MEASUREMENTS

Approx 46 x 56"/117 x 142cm

GAUGE

11 sts and 6 rows = 4"/10cm over double crochet using size J-10 (6mm) hook.
TAKE TIME TO CHECK YOUR GAUGE.

AFGHAN

With A, ch 112.
Row 1 Dc in 4th ch from hook and each ch across—110 dc.
Row 2 Ch 3 (counts as dc throughout), dc in each st across.
Rep row 2 working stripe pat 3 times as foll:
6 rows in A, 2 rows in B, 2 rows in A, 2 rows in B, 6 rows in A, 2 rows in C, 2 rows in A, then 2 rows in C.
Rep row 2, work 6 more rows in A.

BORDER

Rnd 1 Join A in 1st st of foundation ch with sl st, ch 3, 2 dc in same st, work 2 dc in end of each row, work 3 dc in corner, dc in each st across, work 3 dc in corner, work 2 dc in end of each row, work 3 dc in corner, dc in each foundation ch across, join with sl st in top of ch-3, fasten off.
Rnd 2 Join B with sl st in same st as join, ch 3, 3 dc in each corner st, dc in each st around, join with sl st in top of ch-3, fasten off.
Rnd 3 Rep rnd 2 with C. ■

Basics of Crochet

There's no substitute for a hands-on teacher, but our step-by-step primer is the next best thing. So pick up a hook and some yarn, get yourself comfortably seated and let the fun begin!

It all starts with a slipknot.

SLIPKNOT 1

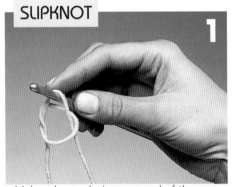

Make a loop, placing one end of the yarn centered underneath the loop. Insert the hook under the center strand and pull it up into a loop on the hook. Pull both yarn ends to tighten the knot on the hook.

FOUNDATION CHAIN 1

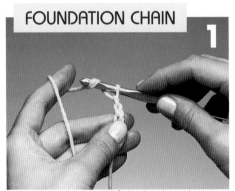

Place the head of the hook under the long end of the yarn. The yarn should lie over the hook from back to front. This is called "yarn over."

SLIP STITCH 1

Insert the hook under both of the top 2 loops of the next stitch and yarn over.

2

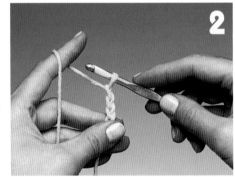

Pull the yarn-over through the loop already on the hook—one chain has been completed.

2

Draw the yarn-over through the stitch and the loop on the hook in one motion.

SINGLE CROCHET

1

Make a foundation chain of desired length. Insert the hook under 2 loops of the next chain stitch and yarn over. (On a foundation row, start in the second chain from the hook.)

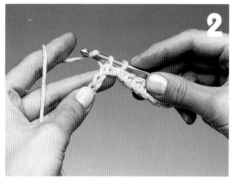

2

Draw the yarn-over through the chain, then yarn over once again. (There are now 2 loops on the hook plus the new yarn-over.)

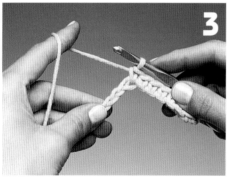

3

Draw the new yarn-over through the 2 loops on the hook—one single crochet completed.

HALF DOUBLE CROCHET

1

To begin a half double crochet stitch, yarn over.

2

Insert hook under the 2 top loops of the next stitch and yarn over.

3

Draw yarn-over through stitch; yarn over again.

4

Draw yarn-over through all 3 loops on hook—one half double crochet completed.

DOUBLE CROCHET

1

To begin a double crochet stitch, yarn over.

1

Insert hook under the 2 top loops of the next stitch and yarn over once again.

3

Draw the yarn-over through the stitch—3 loops are on hook; yarn over once again.

4

Draw yarn-over through first 2 loops; yarn over once again. Draw yarn-over through last 2 loops on hook to complete double crochet.

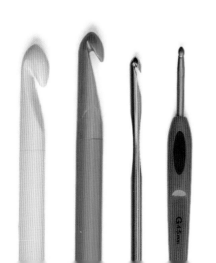

31

my notes